War and Terrorism in International Affairs

War and Terrorism
in International Affairs

Gerardo Jorge Schamís

Translated by Danielle Salti

Foreword by Ben S. Stephansky

132411924

Transaction Books
New Brunswick (U.S.A.) and London (U.K.)

Library of Congress Catalog Number: 79-91346
ISBN: 0-87855-808-X (paper)
Printed in the United States of America

Library of Congress Cataloging in Publication Data

Schamis, Gerardo Jorge.
    War and terrorism in international affairs.

    Translation of Las relaciones internacionales y
la nueva guerra.
    1.   International relations.   2.   War
(International law)   3.   Terrorism   I.   Title
JX1395.S33613   327.1   79-91346
ISBN 0-87855-808-X

Contents

TRANSLATOR'S NOTE

Given the fact that the various passages quoted in the original Spanish-language edition derive from works published in a number of different languages, and for which no references were provided in the original, the use of quotation marks was avoided wherever deemed advisable—in terms of considerations of style, grammatical structure, and the apparent degree of remoteness from any given original text.

Danielle Salti

Foreword

By fortuitous coincidence, at the very time that the editors of *Transaction* were reviewing the final manuscript of this book, a group of experts on terrorism was examining the conditions that form the setting in which this book was written. The experts were assembled in December 1979 by the state of New York's Institute for Studies in International Terrorism and the city of New York's Ralph Bunche Institute on the United Nations. Their main conclusion, headlined in the *New York Times* on December 13, was that "scholars foresee a new age of terrorism"—a conclusion that lends validity to the thesis of this book. Supporting the experts' conclusion was a statistical study of "significant acts" of terrorism during the decade 1970–79 that had been conducted by the state university's institute. Those had risen from 293 in 1970 to 1,511 in 1978, and in the first three months of 1979 alone, 765 such significant acts had been recorded. The grand total for the decade was 6,294 incidents, with 60 percent having occurred in the three-year period of 1977–79. Since the author notes in his preface that he had analyzed some 10 percent of the 1977–78 cases, it is clear from the institute's statistical study that he is writing from an ample data base.

The mounting wave of terrorism during the 1970s sent shock waves throughout the world. But even more alarming was the nature of the terrorist contagion: its almost abrupt appearance; the sweep in scale; its revealed international networks; its diverse uses and technologies bespeaking an emerging "science" of terrorism; and the universal vulnerability to terrorism of both the established nations and those still seeking a stable order.

It is these elements of the terrorist phenomenon that Dr. Gerardo Jorge Schamís addresses in this important and thoughtful book. His message is direct: Terrorism during the past decade has assumed the character of a new form of warfare, taking its place alongside conventional and strategic warfare in the world of international conflict, and its imperfect boundaries with the latter enormously increase the dangers of all three categories. The contemporary world has come to know this new branch of human violence empirically, as it has exploded into an ugly, destructive reality. But where it still eludes sufficient understanding is at the source, where, in the author's language, "the irregular formations, obscure ideology, and generally indistinct objectives, which range from extreme nihilism to the political use of pure violence, confound the analyst and often paralyze the statesman." It is to the source that the reader is pointed, with a review of warfare theory for conceptual guidance, and with a perceptive analysis of the broad frontiers where communist expansionism blends with terrorist warfare to create conditions for a new and more dangerous struggle between the superpowers.

It is the particular virtue of this book that it does not seek the reader's agreement with its thesis or analysis so much as it urgently invites mutual exploration with those who have the responsibility of studying or conducting international relations. Schamís' purpose is to illuminate a subject of baffling complexity and seemingly endless variety of manifestations. The versatility he brings to his study serves us well. He comes to it as teacher and student of law, politics, and international relations; as practical diplomat, twice ambassador for his government; as international civil servant representing the Organization of American States in Europe; and as executive in provincial government. I may be forgiven, therefore, if I find his invitation to reflection irresistable for a comment on the developing world, using as a text Dr. Schamís' observation that terrorism, "this new form of war, (was) born in countries where underdevelopment seems to justify its growth." It seems to me that Dr. Schamís' insightful remark on the birthplace of terrorism suggests a margin of additional treatment concerning the context of the superpower confrontation where Dr. Schamís locates the developing world.

Terrorism may well be the product of the underdeveloped world's revolutions of the 1970s, revolutions bound up with the achievement of real, as against purely formal decolonization. When the imperial powers departed from their colonies after World War II, in most cases government authority was inherited by traditional ruling elites that had served the imperial powers. Some of those elites—Chiang Kai-shek, King Farouk of Egypt, and Emperor Bao Dai of Vietnam—lost power quickly, and a few found constitutional means to share power, but for the most part the elites sought to consolidate their power and enhance it by the work of "modernization."

Both the United States and the Soviet Union played the tutelary role with the traditional elites, and both suffered their share of defeats: for what was building up in the decades after World War II was a growing politicization of Third World societies drawing into national and international politics ever larger numbers of people who increasingly challenged the traditional elites.

The decade of the 1970s was a climactic decade that witnessed the final erosion of the externally tutored elites. It was a decade of revolutions and rebellions riding a crest of mass political movements in Iran, Ethiopia, Pakistan, South Vietnam, Cambodia, Nicaragua, Angola, Mozambique, Rhodesia, South Africa, Nigeria—to name those countries that come to mind—and spilling over into Spain, Portugal, and Greece. What moved the mass political movements was the "right to revolution," which regularly embraced terror, conspiracy, and uprising against oppressive regimes parading as lawful governments under foreign tutelage. The 1970s may well be recorded as one of the most revolutionary decades in history, reproducing on a vast canvas the Jacobin liberationist rationale of the French Revolution, including Robespierre's doctrine of terror that the annihilation of the enemies of the revolution took precedence over formal justice.

If terror was woven into the fabric of the revolutionary 1970s, it has not disappeared with the replacement of the elites by mass politics. That change has brought neither democracy, social justice, nor peace—at least not yet, for most Third World societies remain in states of profound economic dislocation and cultural disorganization. Neither the Soviet Union nor the United States can control the Third World, but it seems inevitable that they will try. This means the Third World's upheavals will draw in the superpowers at what they perceive to be their highest interests. The prospect is further militarization of the birthplace of terrorism, where violence is still an endemic condition.

I trust I have not detained the reader too long with this foreword. I have extended Dr. Schamís' thesis more deeply into the developing world because I believe the greatest danger to the peace of the world is to be found there. The best prescription to meet that danger has recently appeared in the recommendations of the Brandt Commission report. Whether the rich countries, harassed by inflation and deficits, can respond to its proposals for more generous development aid; whether there is a prospect for world agreement on oil prices; or whether disarmament is possible with a heightened superpower struggle—those are the policies that need to be addressed for the developing world if terrorism is not to become an enduring new form of warfare.

Ben S. Stephansky
Carnegie Endowment for International Peace

Preface

The purpose of this work is to evaluate new aspects of
international relations in a world undergoing changes of
unprecedented intensity. We are faced with new situations compelling a fresh analysis of intervening factors at
any given juncture. Those who expect to find innovative
theories or information from secret records will be disappointed, since the value of this work lies in its attempt to
systematize world events—particularly from Western
Europe—disseminated through newspapers, magazines,
and other publications. These include a wide gamut, from
the neofascist *Il Mattino* of Naples to the communist
L'Humanité of Paris, from the rightest *La Croix* to the
social democratic *Le Monde,* the magazine *Der Spiegel*
of Hamburg and the *Atlantic* of Boston, without omit-
ting the *Washington Post* nor the *New York Times.*
There are no secret data; all those mentioned on these
pages have already been made public.

The task has not been easy, above all because the theoretical fundamentals of a new phenomenon are scant and
it is impossible to apply the ancient recommendation of
Lao tse: "He who sees clearly sees from afar." The violent
outburst of terrorism as a totalitarian alternative in the
Western world took many democratic countries, leaders,

and scholars by surprise, and still today, maybe due to the lack of a common analytical framework, there are many who fail to appreciate the dangers hidden behind this new form of war. The only choice is to venture into a mostly empirical analysis and draw conclusions which may not always be correct and will probably be modified in the future, but which may be useful to those engaged in a slower vivisection of this unique phenomenon. As Jacques Bergier states, the world must be warned, by any means within our reach, before it is too late. Western society is in his debt for an enlightening analysis, particularly in his book *World War III Has Begun.*

Perhaps too many facts have been enumerated in this systematization, yet I have only used 10 percent of the data traced, covering 1977 and 1978. Much of the data has also escaped this study, which should be sufficient reason for not reducing its extension. This picture of war constitutes a significant fact of the new world reality, and one of such gravity that it modifies relations within classic international politics. To understand this phenomenon becomes unavoidable for those who have the responsibility of conducting international relations in their respective states.

Hopefully, this work may help to widen the scope of the problem of war—a preliminary and necessary step to activate a reaction which may neutralize the danger threatening all those who have adopted democracy as a political form and as a way of life. This study is directed, particularly, to a sector to which I belong by avocation: the political sector. This deep vocation was aroused more than twenty years ago and applied during all those years toward the analysis of international relations as a starting point to understand the internal process of my own country (Argentina). As Raymond Aron puts it: "Trying to make an in-depth analysis of a country's polity without previously analyzing world reality, is like trying to put on a coat before a shirt."

The reader may wonder why this study lays so much emphasis on the work of the French writer Jacques Bergier, whose mental alertness was not affected by the torture he underwent during World War II and who, being more than seventy years old, is still giving us his full intellectual production. Hopefully, these pages can be a homage to the first writer of universal stature who not only warns about, but also systematizes through scientific analysis the conditions under which new forms of war are developed.

Chapter 1

Political Science, International Relations, and International Politics

From Titus Livius to the present, war has been a very important part of international politics—so much so that many authors, like Jean Baptiste Duroselle, state that war constitutes the very essence of international relations. Even if we admit this to be an exaggeration, it is undeniable that war is a chapter of international politics. War is as old as man, and politics as praxis is equally old. However, as a science, it is a relatively new discipline. During the last few years if has made great progress in developing scientific categories and especially methods of observation. Yet there are several important matters which have remained undetermined. Such is the case for the delimitation of its field of research. It is the question of the autonomy or subordination of political science with regard to other disciplines such as sociology, for example. The problem is so subtle that Duverger even says that the terms *political science* and *political sociol-*

ogy are nearly synonymous. As an example, he mentions American universities, where the same types of problems are regarded as political science when dealt with in departments of political science and as political sociology in departments of sociology.

There are difficulties in establishing the frontiers of a discipline such as political science. Its subject of study covers all social relations mediated by organized power, not only within national communities but also those relations generated by the coexistence of nation-states. Political science studies political phenomena, not only from the point of view of political institutions, history, human geography, economics, etc., but also from a sociological perspective, because all these disciplines are part of the social sciences. It would be absurd to compartmentalize the field of these disciplines since they all have a common point of interest: the life of human beings in its different manifestations. The interrelation among these disciplines is constantly growing, therefore frontiers are extremely subtle. Lipset states that the central subject of political science is not that of establishing its frontiers, but that of serving as a bridge between the normative aspirations of men expressed in their desire to achieve a harmonious society and efforts made by the social sciences to understand the behavior of society from a scientific point of view. There has been greater awareness of the importance of international relations in a world where the interdependence of national communities is increasing. In major universities of the United States, Western Europe, Latin America, and North Africa over the past twenty years, international relations has gained increasing importance in the study of political science.

Rather than argue about the frontiers of these disciplines, it is more important to bear in mind the dynamic character of politics, which is nothing but constant change. This characteristic, added to the importance of juncture and the need for constant interaction with stability, was expressed by Mirabeau in the French Assembly when the famous Declaration of Rights of the Revolution was debated. In one of his speeches he said: "We are not savages just arrived from the shores of the Orinoco to build a society. We are an old nation, maybe too old for our times. We have a preexisting government, a preexisting king. It is necessary to arrange all these things of the revolution and save the suddenness of transit." Politics cannot be measured only in the long run, but also through events and decisions of the juncture, the sum of which contributes to alter or strengthen this long run and make it dynamic as well.

International relations constitute the dynamic conduct of international politics. Ortega y Gasset has often stated that man lives in terms of the future. It is the future which gives meaning to his life and actions. Every activity has its origin, its reason for being, in the achievement of an objective which is an ideal placed at a point in the future, and the shape of the future is based upon that guiding objective which must be understood so that the present may become intelligible. This is so, not only for the individual human being but for the political and social organizations which rule his life and that of the community. The international policies of nations would not be intelligible if we did not bear in mind the objective that each has set as an ideal to conquer, and toward the achievement of which they adopt different actions. These steps, guided by their respective international policy, constitute international relations—subordinate to that policy and also its dynamic element.

War has always been an essential part of international relations; not in vain did von Clausewitz say that war is the continuation of politics by other means. Its study has always been the concern of man, and from Machiavelli to Oscar Wilde it has been analyzed from every point of view: as a political problem (Machiavelli), as a psychological problem, as a cultural problem (Ortega y Gasset and Spengler), as a problem of strategy (von Clausewitz, Beauffré). In our times, war has acquired new characteristics which modify international relations. First, modern instruments of destruction have become deterrents to war, because there is a general awareness that a world collision under present circumstances would result in so great a holocaust that there would be neither winners nor losers. The other reason, which will be our subject of discussion, is what we have called "the new war," unconventional and atypical: international terrorism. This contemporary phenomenon constitutes such an important fact of life that it would be suicide to close our eyes to its manifestations. International relations must also adjust to that new reality. Not understanding this in time could be fatal.

For a better understanding of the new situation generated by universal terrorism as a modern form of war, let us transcribe the reflections made by Gustavo Eichelberg in his work *Man and Technology*. Eichelberg had the felicitous idea of painting the panorama of the social evolution of mankind as a marathon race of sixty kilometers in which each kilometer would be equivalent to ten thousand years. The development of such an extraordinary race has been the following:

The greatest part of the distance to be covered takes place in the jungles without perceptible modifications. Towards the end, when fifty-eight or fifty-nine kilometers have already been covered, there appear the first signs of civilization: the rudimentary utensils of primative man and paintings on the walls of caves. And it is just in the last kilometer that the first farm workers appear. At three hundred meters from the finishing line, the runners make an effort to travel over a road paved with slabs of stone which winds its way to the pyramids of Egypt and the fortifications of ancient Rome. In the last one hundred meters the medieval cities appear; and fifty meters ahead we see a man with intelligent and understanding eyes enthusiastically watching the race: Leonardo da Vinci. There are only ten meters left and they are traveled under the trembling light of torches and oil lamps; but nearly at the end a miracle occurs: the road is flooded with electric light, the carts are replaced by automobiles, and the roar of airplanes can be heard. The runners, astonished, are almost blinded by the powerful floodlights as they are surrounded by reporters. Those last ten meters of the race—along which there have been as many changes as through the enormous preceding period of mankind—represent the last one hundred years. These years are characterized by the fact that the two essential currents of human activity—productive labor and scientific research—have flowed jointly until their waters finally mixed and together they have thrust forward like a flood that transforms everything. This is one of the main reasons for the great acceleration of scientific and technical progress during the past century. Owing to the osmosis of science, production, and technology, man has had the opportunity to exploit the forces of nature, whose potential is unlimited.

This speed of change—also mentioned by Powells in the preface to his book *The Return of the Sorcerers,* where he states that during the last ten years there have been more important qualitative changes than during the last five hundred—is what makes us insist on the need for updating certain concepts which are no longer in force. Where is the classic strategist for our century who discusses, for instance, the subject of terrorism as a form of conflict on a universal scale? The lack of such analysis is why some American universities are emphasizing this field of research.

We are faced with a danger whose gravity has not yet been fully measured. This work hopes to capture the imagination of those who have the responsibility of leadership as well as those who have the responsibility of being governed within the freedom of social critique. If it succeeds in arousing interest in this subject, I will have achieved my aim. It was not my intention to flatter, but rather to warn about dangers and risks, and sometimes this turns out to be unpleasant. Let me recall an episode which Machiavelli relates in *The Prince:* Antiochus went to Greece, summoned by the Aetolians, to fight against the Romans, and he sent ambassadors to the Achaeans who were allied with Rome, to ask them to remain neutral. The Romans, for their part, advised them to take up arms on their side. The Achaeans being assembled while the representatives of Antiochus recommended neutrality, the Roman delegate replied: "As to what is being said regarding the excellence and usefulness of neutrality to your nation, nothing could be more harmful, for if you don't join us you shall, with no consideration or respect whatsoever, be the prize of the winner. He who is not your friend will always advise you to remain neutral, and he who is your friend will ask you to participate in the struggle. Irresolute princes, in order to avoid immediate danger, often prefer to remain neutral, and lose."

Chapter 2

Classic War

War is one of the oldest expressions of international relations. Ever since the first forms of community appeared—such as the clan or tribe—the desire for power, conquest, and survival has caused violent struggles aimed at the achievement of a specific purpose. Through the centuries, this phenomenon has not only continued but has also become a determining factor in the progress of civilization.

The underlying presence of warfare ultimately created its own intimate interaction with a rising society incapable of neutralizing it, and which, paradoxically, made use of war until it became one of the motivations of its technological and scientific development. Such war, called "classic," "typical," or "conventional," reached its climax during 1939-45, and continues up to the present through different conflicts which, though significant, are far less important.

It is almost useless to note the importance of war through the history of mankind. Witness the preoccupation man has shown for framing and defining this activity. In a general sense war is the breaking of peace and the consequent armed struggle among human groups unable to reconcile their differences by way of negotiation. In classic war, the opponents are clearly identified and their struggle develops within certain patterns which govern both parties and to which they try to adhere. But as is the case for most complex human situations whose outcome is grave, definitions are varied and even contradictory, besides being multiple and arising from different social, political, economic, and ideological situations. The Marquis of Olivart, for example, gives a definition which may seem correct at first sight but which, after careful consideration, shows a series of imperfections. In his opinion, "War is a litigation among nations that defend their rights, in which force is the judge and victory the judgment." This reflection is incorrect for several reasons: (1) the belligerents are not always nations; (2) the defense of their rights is not necessarily the "leitmotiv"; (3) war is not a trial; (4) victory is not a judgment but the outcome of a series of factors which join together in favor of the strongest or most skillful.

It may be better to accept the following definition: War is a transitory state of struggle, characterized by an armed and continuous conflict between two or more political communities. This definition of war may be considered ambiguous, but it has the advantage of allowing for civil war to be included in the general concept. Experts have not paid much attention to civil war which has, however, become a matter of great significance during the past few decades, together with terrorism—a new kind of war which has scarcely been considered up to the present. To our definition we could add Clausewitz's statement that "war is the simple continuation of politics by other means," that is to say, "an act of force which compels the opponent to do as we wish," from which it may be inferred that "war is nothing but an extraordinarily amplified combat."

This almost exclusively human activity has attracted the attention of many authors who have wanted to determine its origins, causes, and consequences. From Hugo Crotius and Alberious Gentili to our days, this preoccupation has brought about a great number of definitions and perspectives. Some points of view are extremely descriptive such as those of Funk Brentano and Sorel, who state that war is the political act by which several states, unable to reconcile what they believe to be their duties, rights, or interests, resort to force in order to decide who among them will impose his will on the others. This classic perspective only takes into consideration the struggle among countries. Calvo goes beyond such a framework when he speaks of "an abnormal state of hostility which replaces harmonious relations among nations or citizens belonging to different political parties, the objective being to conquer by force what they have been unable to achieve through peaceful means." Though Calvo considers the case of civil war, we cannot support his criterion that war is merely "an abnormal state of hostility."

Beyond any conceptualizations, classic war has introduced a series of social, economic, and political consequences of increasing complexity corresponding with the intricate net of interests in a developing society. This phenomenon has come to have certain characteristics, unknown until recently, which may be a valid starting point for the analysis and subsequent study of terrorism as a new form of war. Unlike past times, nowadays most struggles involve whole nations. This generates the need to adapt all social manifestations to the existing situation, that is, from the rearrangement of the economic infrastructure—in order to service the needs of the war— to the psychological conditioning of the populations which will suffer its effects. Technological progress, as Erich Fromm points out in *The Anatomy of Human Destructiveness,* has succeeded in leaving no reference picture that can be managed, observed, or adapted to human dimensions. While our eyes and ears receive impressions, the proportions of which are humanly manageable, our concept of the world has lost that quality. This is particularly important as regards the development of modern means of destruction. In modern war a single man can cause the destruction of hundreds of thousands of human beings by just pressing a button. He may not feel the emotional impact of what he is doing since he does not even see or know the people he is exterminating; it is as if there were no connection between the act of pressing the button and the death of those fellow creatures. This wholeness, impersonality, and automatism which characterize war in the final decade of the twentieth century, become important in order to bring out the unusual situation created by terrorist groups in the Western world.

Another preoccupation arising from the existence of war as a social phenomenon has been that of trying to make a juridical characterization of it. Although war constitutes an express violation of the law considered from a modern point of view, legislation relative to war is one of the most polemical and difficult to determine. If we take into account that ethical norms precede juridical rule, we can appreciate the extent to which this particular characteristic of the problem becomes a matter of thorny clarification, and how the political principle predominates over any other type of consideration when dealing with war.

Nearly all traditional religions explicitly condemn war. Jesus told men to put away their swords, for he who draws his sword will be killed by a sword. He also preached that we should love our enemies and "turn the other cheek." This thesis was defended by the heterodox Tertullian when he stated that it was unlawful for Christians to make war. Luther also defended this principle at first, but later, for political reasons, he had to modify the doctrine he had supported—causing the schism. Something similar happened with Muhammad, who first preached meekness and then accepted the jihad (holy war) as a legitimate means—which would allow his followers to determine the future of the West for several centuries. Orthodox Christianism has justified war in certain cases. The clearest expression of this position is that of Father Vitoria, who states that for Christians a just war is a valid war. He based his opinion on Saint Augustine, who stated that if Christian law had considered every war as sinful, it would have commanded all those who wanted salvation to abandon arms; but it just limited itself, through Saint Paul's voice, to saying that soldiers should not protest and should be satisfied with their pay. Saint Thomas said that it is lawful to use weapons against malefactors, secessionists, and foreign enemies. Father Vitoria holds that it is licit to repel the enemy by force and that the verse of the apostle Matthew urging man to turn the other cheek applies to individual cases and not to whole communities. He says that the objective of war is to bring about peace and safety in society, and that a territory having been invaded, it would be offensive to consider that repelling the enemy as well as attacking and disqualifying it for a new aggression, were not a fair procedure.

As far as other fields are concerned, the question of the legitimacy of war and its justification has been dealt with in most dissimilar ways. The most realistic state that armed struggle is a fact—regardless of the right to undertake such action. That is why Hume considered that the violence of war is nothing but the suspension of justice between opposing parties, while others, like Machiavelli, believed that its necessity is what makes it legitimate. Martens observes that the two extreme positions—war considered as a judgment of God (holy) or as a crime— both deny the right to wage war, and that in spite of the arguments that may be put forward, it must always exist. This implies that beyond the violence against preexisting ethical norms and the consequent underlying irrationality, war is ruled by principles which the belligerents must respect, and in the case of nations, their observance will reciprocally bring them the rights recognized by specific laws. This line of thought is the basis of international treaties which attempt to regulate warfare, introducing rules that may humanize an attitude which is, as such, excluded from the principles guiding a civilized society.

This fundamental contradiction has kept legislation in an embryonic state and penalties imposed for the violation of basic human rules are reduced to mere moral repudiation, while in specific military terms technological developments have been astonishing. If we accept that war interrupts a state of law respected until then by opposing parties, we will have a true picture of the limited coercive power of the rules set up for this exceptional situation, rules which will hardly find an organization capable of enforcing them with the utmost rigor.

The simple reading of any of the episodes in history where a state of law based on peace was broken, is conclusive proof of what has been said. The weakness of the laws of war is shown to a superlative degree in the case of a civil war. If the setting of standards is an impossibility when the struggle involves two or more countries compelled to observe preexisting international treaties (Vietnam/China, March 1979), the situation becomes even worse when the struggle is among citizens of the same state bringing about the temporary suspension of guarantees which ruled the life of that society and replacing them with others that are highly arbitrary to the opposing party supposed to observe that new pattern. That is why it is in civil wars where the fighting cruelty clearly manifests itself, sometimes becoming an extermination attempt on both sides where the prisoner has no guarantees at all. General José de San Martín was preoccupied by this very matter when he urged the congressmen of Tucumán (Argentina) to declare independence, since such a decision would bring about the rule of international law over the struggles taking place in that part of South America. This was a matter of great importance since while civil wars— and in many ways this was one—as such are foreign to international law, they do fall within its theoretical jurisdiction once the opponents have established their government and have their own army—to the extent that such an attitude would establish the division of the state into two or more parts none of which would have enough power for the full exercise of its prerogatives and sovereignty.

The most serious problem civil wars bring to international law is the recognition of the state of belligerency of the party which has risen against the established government. This recognition is very important because, aside from the fact that taking the cause to be just and the struggle to be serious implies moral support, it compels the country granting such recognition to adopt an equidistant position, that is to deal with both opponents in the same way. The clearest example of the consequences that may derive from this type of conflict is the Spanish Civil War, which had a direct involvement in the international policies of the time, to the extent of becoming the antechamber of World War II, as Julio Alvarez del Bayo, former prime minister of the Republic, states in his work *Everything Begins in Spain.*

These reflections aim at showing the contradictions and ambiguities of war, causing the reactions of mankind to this aspect of international relations—and even of domestic policies—to be widely dissimilar. Apologists such as Spengler deny the possibility of achieving world peace, emphasizing the immanent nature of man which blocks the way to that alternative. Spengler states that life is a struggle without respite among plants, animals, and men; a struggle among individuals; and among military, political, and social classes. It is a fiery struggle for power to carry out one's own will or one's own idea of what is just or useful and, if other means fail, force will always be used as an ultimate resource. An individual who uses violence may be regarded as a criminal, a social class as revolutionary or treacherous, a nation as bloody—but none of those facts changes the problem. In our day, world communism speaks of its wars as revolutions; colonial empires speak of the pacification of foreign nations; and if the world were a union of states, wars would be spoken of as revolutions. These are mere verbal differences. Spengler also says that the strong and unspent races are not pacifist. This would amount to a denial of the future, because the pacifist ideal implies a final condition which is in contradiction with one fact: as long as there is human development, there will be war.

Spengler's pessimistic though apologetic view had also been that of many illustrious predecessors like Heraclitus, who considered war to be creative and the beginning of all things; or like Hegel who stated that it is beautiful, good, holy, and fecund; it creates the morality of peoples and it is indispensable for maintaining moral health. It is at war that the state comes closest to its ideal, because it is then the life and possessions of citizens are most closely subordinated to the preservation of the common entity.

At the other end of the spectrum, those who attack war on the basis of a social and political doctrine whose ideal is to suppress war by means of a juridical organization for peace, are no less in number. Since ancient times, great writers and philosophers have supported this position. There is the famous statement by Herodotus, for example, that nobody can be so insensate as to prefer war to peace; in times of war parents bury their children, in peacetime it is the children who bury their parents. Aristotle, Horace, Ovid, and Seneca, among other classical thinkers, abound in recriminations against war, but these are often too poetic or philosophical in character to reverse the status quo. From Dante, Montaigne, Pascal, and Rousseau (who said that war was the most abominable enemy that hell had ever spewed) to Jean Jaurès or

Bertrand Russell, there have always existed pacifist spirits ready to prove their theories. While being president of the United States of America, Wilson tried to crystallize his preaching but failed. The reason may perhaps lie within a certain idealism which all opponents to war have in common. They all assume that the evolution of man moves toward the elimination of such a scourge and that the only thing needed is to set rules that may aid or complement that natural process. This line of thought and action which gathered increasing strength at the turn of the century, gave rise to the creation of the League of Nations after World War I and finally weakened when it failed to reconcile definite interests. Its successor, the United Nations, has also been incapable of eliminating or even reducing the tendency toward conflict.

In this brief enumeration of the supporters of peace it is impossible not to mention Juan Bautista Alberdi, a true precursor of an organization of nations through his work *The Crime of War*. The Englishman C.T. MacConnell has said that if *The Crime of War* had been published in French in Paris, London, or Berlin instead of appearing in Latin America, it would have created a sensation, achieved wide circulation in numerous editions, and would have received the subtitle of *Gospel of Peace*. In this work Alberdi states that war is the right to commit a crime, a dreadful and sacrilegious contradiction, and a sarcasm against civilization.

The technological and scientific developments of the final decades of our century suggest an appreciable change which will have to be taken increasingly into account. We may even have to reconsider the principles sustained up to the present for and against warfare or to meditate upon a reality which, in this as in other fields of human experience, is no longer thoroughly understandable from the viewpoint of traditional thinking. It is the first time that such a remarkable stock of destructive weapons is being accumulated; weapons which will never be used unless the desired outcome be the destruction of the civilized world and probably the annihilation of most of the inhabitants of this planet. A global war under these circumstances would have no absolute winners, thus eliminating one of the fundamental motivations of any armed conflict. This appears to be the only reason to be considered within a hypothesis of coexistence which, however, can hardly be understood as peaceful for it lacks a fundamental element: what the Romans called "animus."

Whatever one's ideological perspective, it is a fact that the Soviet regime is essentially expansive. This raises the question of whether expansion can be reconciled with peace. The dialogue between the two contemporary superpowers is nothing but a renewed application of the old "armed peace." Such coexistence is not based on ethical principles but on the threat of the dead end of absolute risk.

Proof that this unusual element has entered the world of international relations can easily be provided by taking into account only two facts: (1) the arms race has not stopped; (2) pacts between the two big powers are updated or readjusted periodically. If we analyze United States and Soviet developments after World War II, when they were allies, we find that the warfare industry continues to be the most important dynamic basis of both economies, and that arms technology has developed more rapidly than other industrial activities. A very important detail which is often overlooked is that during the past decades, the Soviet Union has given special priority to its offensive arsenal, emphasizing the most sophisticated weaponry such as rockets. Their total arms expenditure represents 13 percent of Soviet gross national product—their growth being between 4 and 5 percent per annum in terms of constant values, thus exceeding the rate of growth for the economy as a whole. This would be enough to confirm the thesis about Soviet expansionism, but there are other elements to be considered. The dissimilar production of strategic weapons brings about the periodic readjustment of the SALT treaties, despite the initial assumption that they were to last for several decades. These negotiations dealing with strategic armaments have until now ignored traditional non-nuclear armaments. The price of such an omission could be high for the West, maybe excessively dazzled by that eventual coexistence on an absolute level which has made the relative realm even more so. While many Western statesmen, politicians, and experts were paying renewed attention to the endless series of discussions of SALT II, French intelligence was dousing cold water on Western Europe. The conclusions arrived at by the French showed that the forces of the Warsaw Pact needed only forty-eight hours to prepare a large-scale surprise attack on that part of the continent. If that forecast was correct—and there is no reason to doubt it—we are dealing with a military organization of astonishing efficiency, not only because of the quantity and quality of the armaments but also because of its overwhelming superiority. It is known, for example, that during the past ten years the number of

Soviet divisions in the European continent have increased by 20 percent, the total military personnel by 40 percent, and land armaments by 30 percent. The imbalance regarding tanks would be of 55,000 to NATO's 17,000, and in terms of airplanes 8,000 for the Pact as opposed to merely 3,500 for the Western countries.

That enormous accumulation of forces threatening the heart of the world would lack real strategic effectiveness if the final intention of the Soviets were to launch it as an explosive offensive in the German blitzkrieg manner of 1939. Such foolishness would consolidate no power. It would just annihilate all known ones in a few hours. What is then the objective of that threat? If we take a close look at the map of the world and its geopolitical fluctuations after World War II, we find a suitable approximation to the truth or a very interesting working hypothesis. The nuclear deterrent which prevents a significant conflict in the central countries determined that the liberation of warlike tensions would be transferred to peripheral areas of the world in search of positional advantages which would ultimately lead to negotiations, on better grounds, around a hegemonic project or at least a fairly stable parity. In this regard, the Soviets have shown a very special quality, so much so that Harry and Bonaro Overstreet, in their work *The Essence of Communism,* define it as a strange force, the strangest and most enigmatic in all history, and which, in just forty years, has taken possession of one-third of the inhabitants and one-fourth of the territories of the world. A state which learned the peculiar art of practicing totalitarianism at home and fractional conquest abroad, offers itself to the world as the vanguard of peace, liberation, and anti-imperialism. The most recent examples thoroughly prove this. Through attacks and counterattacks varying in importance but generally favorable, the Soviet Union has extended its power to highly sensitive geopolitical regions. The African battle (using Cuba), the Indo-Chinese expansionism through Vietnam (stopped for the time being by its worst enemy—China), and interference in the Persian Gulf (Iran) and Central Asia, all account for a convergent tactic insinuated from the periphery to the center. The methods are multiple and subtle, comprising an integral strategy which may have a warlike, economic, or cultural basis.

Classic war may be an anachronism for the central countries and a constant threat for the peripheral ones; but every hegemonic project inevitably aims at the heart or brain of the opposing system, or of the remaining opponent having enough power and reserves to cause one's own project to fail. And if the end justifies the means, these must be carefully dosed in order to undermine the enemy's capabilities and prevent an untimely reaction to cause one's scheme to fail. An all-out conflict thus laid aside, war can no longer be understood as "a transitory state of conflict characterized by an armed and continuous struggle among two or more political communities." Modern war has lost that quality, that absolute simplicity, and has come to have a new character more suited to our times. It is now a subtle network of economic, social, political, and ideological offensives, shifting its military angle to a dimension which acts as a catalyst of these elements and, at the same time, contains them in itself. We are facing a new form of war: terrorism.

Terrorism, in the systematic and organized way in

which it is carried out today, is the typical outcome of a society which seems to have lost vigor in the ideological-philosophical sphere yet exhibits an unsurpassed capability as regards scientific and technological innovation. Such a conceptual breakdown together with an expansionism which generates crises and sociopolitical or socioeconomic readjustments implying a defensive strategy against such totalitarian advance, has resulted in the recreation of a violent phenomenon supplementary to conventional warfare and adapted to the conditions or rules of an "armed peace" which—artificial or not—the world will attempt to maintain at all cost.

In the past, truces agreed to by two opposing armies had a military rather than political objective. Negotiations between the belligerents were a pretext for reorganizing their forces and planning new offensive or defensive maneuvers. In this sense, the atomic truce is no different from traditional ones. Its main characteristic is that reorganization is dissuasive and combat is not held in the military field but in alternative ones: the political, ideological-cultural, and terrorist fields. In this way, the expansive strategy tends to gradually close the fence or at least weaken defenses. "Violence spreads from the periphery to the heart of civilization." This statement appeared in a work called "Response to Violence" which was the result of a study carried out by a French commission headed by Alain Peyrefitte with the participation of Raymond Aron and Jean Fourastier, among others. The conclusion does not seem to raise many objections, but it must be taken into account as much as other tactics which converge on the same objective. Eurocommunism—a position which cannot sustain a serious analysis because of the very inconsistency of the phenomenon as such— must not be overlooked in its effects by the leaders of democracy.

In an interview by *Información Latina* in Paris in April 1978, Peyrefitte stated that Eurocommunism was an entelechy and an artificial creation. "There is only one communism," he said, "whether the subsidiary be in Rome or in Lima. To think in such terms, as many newspapers of Western Europe do, is dangerously ingenuous." Four years ago, and forty-eight hours before the election which would confront Giscard d'Estaing with Mitterand for the second time, George Marchais, secretary general of the French Communist party, announced on television that if the union of the Left triumphed over the opposition, his party would take over the departments of education and defense. The effect was instantaneous. Many French mothers became frightened at the idea of an eventual communist education for their children and voted against Mitterand. The same happened to many voters who sympathized with the Center-Left or had vacillated up to that moment and who would never accept that France abandon NATO and join the Warsaw Pact. Was Marchais's attitude a coincidence or a provocation? Was the intention to frustrate the Socialist leader's triumph because it would not suit Moscow's interests? This should be enough to prove that Communist parties have not shown their divorce from the Soviet Union to be real, and that their claimed ideological autonomy is in fact part of a whole strategy which combines a political bridgehead with a military threat of unsuspected destructive effects.

Chapter 3

New Forms of War

World War II was the final chapter of a conventional war of great significance. The ghost of total and maybe permanent destruction established the delicate balance of armed peace, a subterfuge which has facilitated the creation of new styles of warfare, the most dangerous of which is organized terrorism. This new form of war, unknown until not long ago, has transformed an important part of the Western world into its battlefield, arousing confusion among the most brilliant statesmen, politicians, and military confronted with situations which must be faced quickly and empirically.

If it was difficult to define conventional war in the past—in spite of existing knowledge and the attention paid to the problem—it will be very hard to frame this new element almost abruptly incorporated into the West. The most suitable definition for this new type of warfare may yet be that which Machiavelli used to define war in general, as the action performed by one group against another and aiming at its extermination. But we do not always know who is on one side and who on the other and furthermore, they do not always exhibit the same characteristics. This conceptual ambiguity to explain such a complex phenomenon (perhaps due to his skeptical view of man rather than to loose judgment) is still the one which best illustrates the substantive characteristics of terrorism. Irregular formations, obscure ideology, generally indistinct objectives which range from extreme nihilism to the political use of pure violence, this new form of war born in countries where underdevelopment seems to justify its growth, is now attacking nations at the highest level of the Western world, thus forcing a review of any hasty concepts about its causes.

To date, theoretical contributions have been sparse. The Military School of Saint Cyr attempted to provide some scientific basis in its analysis of this new type of war when it studied certain outbreaks in Indochina and Algeria which endangered French national security. Other organizations engaged in the study of strategic-military or intelligence problems have, compelled by circumstances, begun to dig into the characteristics of this phenomenon and its significance to the juridical, economic, social, political, geopolitical, and other fields. Some European and North American universities (Georgetown University, for example) have also carried out research on this subject. In a very specific course on international relations, the International University of Florida (Miami) discussed the social, economic, and political life of contemporary Europe and the European reply since 1968 in Paris. This shows that the term *terrorism* is a recognized entity in a number of centers for the study of international relations as an important element of the present Western world.

This new concern has found a precocious thinker in

Jacques Bergier, one of the most prolific writers of our time and a famous investigator of sociopolitical and socioeconomic subjects. Bergier has made very important contributions through several conferences held in Europe and Japan and, above all, through his work *World War III Has Begun,* written and published in 1976. As he sees it, in the fight against subversive terrorism, analysts, intellectuals, writers, and so forth have one fundamental task: to predict the future. It does not matter whether this analysis needs to be corrected or adjusted periodically as a result of a mistaken appreciation or a necessary modification of the tactics used. What is important is the sustained warning of the danger posed by the internationalization of this war, thereby preventing it from spreading, as a lethal stigma, over the whole planet.

Bergier's analysis is the most important to date, even though his forecasts have not been wholly accurate. The reason for his mistakes may be found in two factors: (1) the contributions of various authors had effective repercussions and fulfilled the very valuable function of warning security organizations and reticent politicians about this new situation; (2) in spite of having appeared in Paris during the events of 1968, terrorism used Latin America and similar peripheral areas as grounds for experimentation, allowing other states to gain the necessary experience for improving their own security systems. Thus, as regards this defensive as well as offensive organization, West Germany stands now as the leading nation, owing to the collaboration of responsible sectors of NATO and also because the German parliament authorized the use of the necessary funds for that purpose.

· However, those measures should have been taken

when the iron was hot, when the situation showed that it was impossible to go on acting according to traditional methods. This, together with the celerity of events in the field of subversive terrorism, has made Bergier's work lose its force regarding many of its conclusions, but not in terms of his experience, research, and descriptions of events in some European countries, which are still very useful. *World War III Has Begun* attracted the attention of specialists and raised the awareness of responsible sectors, resulting in a decision to deal very seriously with a problem involving the survival of democracy.

Bergier points out that World War III (the terrorist war) has already begun and what is worse, the West is losing. At the time, more than two years ago, he seemed to be right. Today, in light of the systematization of data, we could state that, at least, the West is no longer losing. It is important to go over Bergier's work from a critical point of view, because it helps to clarify the alleged polemic as to the final outcome of events.

If the terrorists' plans had been carried out in accordance with Bergier's forecasts, West Germany would have been the first country to succumb. Bergier is aware that this opinion may seem incredible or even fantastic. He admits that people have a right to ask themselves how Germany might have yielded to the attacks of only a few thousand native leftists, Marxist Palestinians, and discontented Japanese, when thirty years ago the three biggest world powers had to join forces to defeat that nation. According to Bergier, had Germany not defended itself energetically, a few years later the chaos would have been such that the administration of that state would have become a de facto and de jure impossibility. Had this happened, troops from East Germany would have intervened in order to protect their country against such a threat, and nobody would have opposed that intervention because it would have been made in the name of order and security, very dear to European nations and, above all, to the German people. Bergier says that at that time (before 1976), West Germany had become accustomed to giving in to terrorists. They were set free whenever possible. Until then, the only attempt at resistance had occurred in Stockholm. Bergier takes as an example the kidnapping of German politician Peter Lorenz which took place on February 27, 1975. Lorenz was the candidate for Christian Democracy in the municipal elections of West Berlin. He was threatened with murder unless five terrorists were set free. Germany agreed. After having been freed, Lorenz declared to the newspaper *Minute* that those people were destructive intellectuals whose only dream was cataclysm. The only way to stop their action quickly was to attack them and in order to do this the legal scope of action of police would have to be expanded for a short time. He added that he was convinced that people would accept such restrictions which would, by themselves, maintain freedom.

Before Lorenz's kidnapping, terrorists from the world over walked freely around Germany, but it was from that moment onward that they strengthened their activities. This was perhaps the reason why some defensive measures began to be adopted, such as the creation of an anti-terrorist service directed by Gerhard Boeden, former guard to Kissinger, composed of only 180 men. This service was enlarged and today it includes about 4,000 highly qualified personnel and its management is autarchic.

Another problem was that the German police did not

have an antiterrorist information service and, to obtain such data, it relied upon the French police. On the other hand, its opponents had many excellent "friends" in their organization, some of them old Nazis who even had enough influence to get their men set free. One of the most famous cases is that of Siegried Haag, former attorney to the "Baader band," supplier of weapons and accomplice in the attack on the German Embassy in Stockholm in April 1975. Haag was arrested in Heidelberg and set free almost immediately. Why? It is not known. Afterwards, it was found out that he had rented a residence in Saint Jean de Bueges, France, and that he was living there with his wife. At that time, Bergier stated that the group, which he called Interterror (international organization of terrorism), was going to attempt a big coup to set the Baader band free. He added that they were going to achieve their purpose. This pessimistic forecast did not turn out to be true. However, it is impossible not to agree with Bergier as to a certain passivity, nearly suicidal, of security forces. On August 18, 1975 the French newspaper *Le Point* stated that those men were preparing a big job. It was said that they were getting ready to obtain radioactive substances in order to extort by threatening with pollution. It was going to be the life of rivers and lakes in exchange for the freedom of Andreas Baader and his three assistants. *Le Point* concluded that it was a crazy matter though not unthinkable. As Bergier states, it was evident that the German police did not read *Le Point*—neither did it pay any attention to the press of its own country which was demanding the arrest of the murderers of Judge Günther von Drenkamnn, with no

results. Yet when old Nazis were arrested by chance—
men who might have revealed secrets dangerous to
terrorism—they were unfailingly found hanging in their
cells, whilst those accused of subversive activities
received Jean-Paul Sartre and other sympathetic person-
alities. This was what made Bergier exclaim that Germany was losing the battle and so was the West. What
reasons led to this situation? Bergier—who was tortured
by the Nazi special services during World War II—
believes it is because the German nation is still shocked by
the actions of the Gestapo and is not willing to accept a
strong police, rejecting any form of repression that may
bring back to mind those terrible events. This would
explain why the *Red Star* of Frankfurt remained undis-
turbed, despite the fact that the owner of the plant,
Johannes Weinrich, had rented the car which on January
13, 1975 was used by Palestinian terrorists to attack Orly
Airport. Those involved in the affair were later sent by
plane to Libya. Until then, France had not understood
the importance of the threat either, but after the "Carlos
affair" (which will be referred to later on) its eyes were
opened.

From 1976 onward—maybe as a result of the Baader
band's attack in Stockholm the year before, following
instructions by the Brazilian Carlos Marighela (who died
in 1969) in his *Minihandbook of the Urban Guerrilla*—
political forces in Germany seemed to understand the
seriousness of the matter. Marighela's handbook is being
studied by police forces over Europe, and the Germans
are taking some security measures which still lack realism
(too little too late). By then, Bergier states that security

forces were multiplying their optimistic announcements assuring, on every occasion, that they had exterminated the last twenty terrorists. Famous last words.

But if Germany is a battlefield—says Bergier—France is a field for experimentation. This would neither be a novelty nor a casual choice. During the Spanish Civil War, the weapons to be used in World War II were tested in that country. According to Bergier, the geographic locale for the tests has now been changed in order to test the psychological and physical tactics needed for this new war. Thus, we should understand: (1) the total social disorganization of May 1968; (2) the gratuitous attack, conceived as a simple act of terror; (3) the murder of two policemen and the simultaneous execution of a traitor member of Interterror; (4) the holding of a meeting, at the end of April 1975, to analyze the situation. On May 28, 1975, the newspaper *Minute* stated that, aside from the habitual representatives of MIL, ETA, the Communist Revolutionary Front (ultra-Maoist), and GARI, the representatives of the French branch of the former German red forces (alias "Baader band" and "June 2nd Movement") were, for the first time, present at that meeting.

To Bergier all said movements were synchronized since the Havana Conference. He says one can laugh when the French interior minister, Raymond Marcellin, speaks of an international conspiracy, but he is right. During 1975, Japanese, Marxist Palestinian, Dutch, German, Spanish, Portuguese, and other organizations were working in France. There were also French organizations composed of youths who were under twenty years of age and who regreted that they could not belong to the OAS because they were too young. These young groups were supplied with money and arms by Interterror, which was organizing them. By that time they trained by attacking leaders of the NDR or of the Socialist party. Bergier points out that for Interterror, the French passports which these youths were able to obtain were highly useful, allowing them to travel through several countries thus being able to carry arms, money, etc. In his opinion, they numbered only a few thousand, that is to say, in numbers they could not be compared to the Resistance or to the OAS. He also says that none of the youths believed they were working to take over power in France. Up to that moment (toward the end of 1976) they were obeying orders from their Japanese, Palestinian, or German Marxist leaders, with an iron discipline. They did not seem to have clear ideas as to the future, but that did not prevent them from organizing an attack upon an atomic plant. Though the objective of the takeover of France was not clearly expressed, Bergier believed it implied a culminating point of World War III. Both from the point of view of prestige and eventual sacking, France would be a unique target.

At that time Bergier believed that the destruction of France as a state, its occupation by Eastern troops, and the elimination of French colonies in the Third World would be events comparable to Hitler's victory of 1940, and that this goal could be achieved with very limited means and with a French participation inferior in quantity and quality to the Nazi column which had acted on that occasion. He was also afraid that no politicians were fully aware of the situation.

Those victories which Bergier viewed as very likely to take place in Germany and France also filled him with dark thoughts concerning Italy, because of the increasing internal disorganization of the peninsula. Rival organizations, directly controlled by Interterror in the case of the Left and indirectly governed by neofascism in the case of rightist groups, were engaged in a struggle characterized by the impunity with which they performed their actions. Kidnappings and attacks carried out by a terrorism which felt encouraged by the very passivity and disorder of the state became regular events. For Bergier this situation raised two alternatives: if Interterror succeeded in achieving its purposes in France and Germany, Italy would fall like a ripe fruit. Otherwise, the Mafia could increasingly intervene in order to stop the chaos, acting as a substitute for the authority which was not being exercised by the constituted powers.

The only country that seemed aware of the immediate danger was England. Although Interterror had skillfully taken advantage of the Irish Civil War in order to extend its action toward the islands and thus disguise attacks against the civil population, it has perhaps—says Bergier—made the same mistake Hitler made, acting prematurely. By that time, the efficiency of the secret services of the British police had already begun to produce significant results. Thanks to such services it was possible to have an idea of the methods and objectives of international terrorism. The British got ready to fight against this scourge following the implacable tactics used by Israel. They established special antiterrorist forces on the basis of military groups drawn from the Second Special Regiment of the Air Force, while the army organized three special branches in the Ministry of Defense: (1) the

MACP, giving military support to the police which essentially lacks armaments and is small in number; (2) the MACC, providing helicopters for specific operations, and (3) the MACM, which is in charge of air transport and protection equipment should it be necessary to transfer a ministry or a governmental team. Another measure which was being studied was joining the three branches of the intelligence service: the special branch of Scotland Yard, the D15 office in charge of internal security, and the D16 which deals with foreign information. By that time, the British army was already in a state of premobilization and ready to defend itself or attack subversive groups.

Yet as Bergier points out, British authorities considered these measures to be insufficient, especially as regards identification of the enemy to be attacked. That is always the real problem. It was thought that most terrorist attacks were not carried out by the Irish or by sympathizers of their cause, of British nationality. They were actually carried out by Japanese, Germans, or Palestinians who camouflaged their real intentions taking advantage of the regional conflict. The weapons used in those attacks were proof of that double origin. There were Armalite AR15 rifles, manufactured in Japan under United States license and supplied to the IRA by the United States Committee of Aid to Ireland, as well as explosive materials obtained from a clandestine plant near Dublin discovered in April 1975. But there also appeared Kalatchnikoff rifles (Soviet), SAM antiaircraft rockets, and bombs manufactured in Czechoslovakia. This proved Interterror's intervention in the conflict. Yet

Bergier was of the opinion that their opposing objectives would, sooner or later, separate both groups and prevent them from complementing each other.

Bergier believed that the advantage the British had over other European countries in terms of handling this type of war was that both the government and the people were aware of its consequences. According to Bergier, that attitude was invaluable because it allowed the timely adaptation of the means of combat.

This review of Bergier's analysis published in 1976 purports to renew the picture of the situation beyond that date. Events have shown that there does exist an international organization which controls and supervises terrorist activities carried out the world over. That is why the name Interterror is more than an arbitrary intellectual elucubration. We are faced with an unusual type of war which can hardly be handled according to the principles of traditional strategy, not only in the military but also in the political field. Regarding this latter field it is also indispensible to adopt new means of fighting Interterror, whose methods may not be considered unknown in terms of isolated cases, but which are indeed unknown if we take into account its significance as a world organization with powerful allies. Interterror resembles the image of the iceberg, of which this international organization is merely the visible part. The real problem is hidden.

Chapter 4

Terrorism in Europe

Bergier's hypotheses on the existence of a "superior intelligence" coordinating the presumably independent operations of the different terrorist groups, left the speculative sphere after the publication of his work. From 1976 onward this new form of war vigorously broke out in Western European countries betraying its real objectives and forcing governments to action.

In March 1978, the Red Brigades (Italian ultraleftist group) kidnapped Christian Democratic leader Aldo Moro. They intercepted his car in Rome, in broad daylight, killed his five guards, and successfully eluded a 55-day manhunt—concluding their action by shooting the prisoner. Six months earlier, the German anarchist group Baader-Meinhof carried out an identical plan to kidnap industrialist Hans Schleyer. They shot his four guards, ridiculed police for forty-three days, and ended their work by killing the businessman. It was not the first time these groups had kidnapped or killed. In Italy, Moro was the twelfth victim in 1978; in Germany, Schleyer was the tenth in 1977. In a decade of spectacular violence, crimes such as these have lost the impact they would have had a few years ago. What was astonishing in both cases was the terrorist technique: cold-blooded, decisive, precise, and logistically admirable. Everything had been foreseen within a framework of security and impunity.

The actions against Moro and Schleyer were not casual. They had been carefully planned as part of an itinerary of terror which covered all Europe—the Red Brigades called it "operational cooperation." Proof of this is the document called "Resolution on the Strategic Course," which was made public after Moro's kidnapping. This is a work written by experts in revolutionary Marxism whose supreme objective, as declared by Renato Curcio—leader of the Red Brigades—is "the final European war for the achievement of communism." Germany and Italy, "the strongest and weakest links in the Western democratic system," are viewed as states placed in the front line of such a war, their terrorists being the elite batallions of an international communist army. The kidnappings of Moro and Schleyer were planned to promote the organization of that continental force; and their future actions would be intended to unify the different European groups into a single Organization for Communist Combat which would aim its blows at the "vital centers of Western multinational imperialism."

Had the Red Brigades spoken about mass movements or political parties, their magnificent strategy would have been utopian. But the international terrorist organization they allude to is much more modest—although it already has troops all over Europe. Spread over the whole continent, they show a tendency toward nationalism, separatism, anarchism, Maoism, and Leninism, with one common denominator: an ultraleftist ideology of armed revolution as a means to bring about the destruction of the system. These groups, which may be small or large, active or latent, work together for the achievement of their purpose in different places of the world, unifying their interests on behalf of a common identity.

For the time being, the Moro and Schleyer affairs are but elementary studies on how to destabilize a country; how to keep a state "enclosed" on account of a rescue; how to paralyze police action; how to frighten the population. The cold calculation behind these attacks suggests that the worst is yet to come. The state of alert imposed upon Europe by NATO scarcely a month after the assassination of Moro was the result of an explicit warning by West German security officers, afraid of terrorist extortion: a raid on a warehouse of nuclear bombs, kidnapping of officials, stealing of raw materials, occupation of plants, etc.

Is Europe moving in this direction? Are the terrorists sufficient in number to accomplish their strategy? For how long can they maintain a clandestine life eluding the largest police system established since Nazism? Where do they get the money, arms, training, hideouts, and orders? Is it perhaps too late to stop them? These are some unanswered questions.

There is a difference between "bona fide" terrorists and the numerous European radical "autonomists" (students and workers on the Left of Communist parties). The autonomists ("l'idiot servant" according to *L'Express*) carry arms, hurl Molotov cocktails during riots, and even cover up some terrorists. Most terrorists are recruited from autonomist groups, but the aim of autonomists is not murder. Terrorists do not glorify death either, they view it as a means. They apply the old Chinese proverb: "Kill one, frighten ten thousand." They need not be sharpshooters since in most cases they aim at the legs, cripple their victims, then go for the heart or head. A silencer, a few months' practice, and the *Official Handbook of the Swiss Army* (a 6,000-copy edition was sold out in Italy) are generally enough.

The surprising thing is that, being relatively few in number, they can cause so many deaths. In Northern Ireland, during nine years of implacable guerrilla struggle, there have been about four hundred murders. This number is proportionately smaller than in countries like Italy, Germany, or Spain (the latest battlefield). According to Italy's minister of the interior, the Moro operation—the planning of which required one year and two million dollars—employed no more than sixty members of the Red Brigades, including "irregular" assistants and sharpshooters (at most half a dozen). The general idea that they have many "specialists" has, in many cases, been created by the action of the same group hiding its identity by means of wigs, beards, glasses, etc., and skillfully managing in traffic (powerful automobiles with movable automatic license plates, police sirens, frequency radios).

According to Italian and German authorities, the total number of terrorists who can handle a gun does not exceed three hundred. What they do have is large financial resources. They generally get them by "expropriating" funds through kidnappings or bank holdups. It is also a way of gaining experience. The business is clear: a single kidnapping (that of a rich man from Genoa in 1977) was more than enough to cover the expenses of the Red Brigades for the Moro operation. An Italian officer declared to *Oggi* that they are extremely rich, as are their German comrades. There are also some differences between both groups: the Red Brigades seem to be more

spartan than the Baader-Meinhof band, the June 2nd
Movement, and the faction of the Red Army. Ulrike
Meinhof—who committed suicide more than two years
ago while in prison—and her group almost spoiled relations with the Palestinian Marxist terrorists when com-
plaining of the rudimentary comfort of the Middle East
training camps. It seems that their tastes became more
sophisticated as their funds increased: fifty-five million
dollars obtained from kidnappings and robberies since
1970, according to authorities. Another remarkable difference is the greater precautions the Germans take
regarding security, despite the fact that lately both organizations have been restricted by the autonomists in their
collaboration, maybe because they were afraid or simply
because they were opposed to the way in which the
Schleyer and Moro affairs were handled. This has compelled the Red Brigades to be more careful, thus proving
that any subversive organization needs at least some
social consensus in order to survive.

The commonalities among these groups are many and
this is natural. The way in which they are formed and
trained is similar and their leaders are intelligent and
sophisticated; they are college-trained intellectuals, usu-
ally brighter than their peers. Renato Curcio, for example, was the star of the Department of Sociology at the
University of Trento; while Ulrike Meinhof was the spoilt
child of "chic" radical journalism in Germany. When they
became clandestine in 1970, they already had a solid theoretical background, and were thoroughly informed of
revolutionary Marxist thought.

Their ideological extraction has two origins: the reli-
gious Left and Communist parties or their variants. The
Red Brigades are half former Catholics and half former

Communists. Ulrike Meinhof and many of her group are former Protestants and Communists. They have all read the works of Ché Guevara, Régis Debray, and even the handbooks of the Tupamaros. Moreover, the revolutionary history of Europe is a very important teacher: there is an undeniable similarity between today's terrorist tactics, displayed in Rome or Berlin, and those which the pre-Bolshevik Russian nihilists used to assassinate Czar Alexander II and three thousand of his policemen during the past century.

Much of the speculation surrounding Italian and German terrorists is fantasy. They do not inevitably need "Moscow's gold" to operate. They can, on their own, buy or steal any number of weapons or explosives; they have their own printing press to forge passports and identity cards as well as their own molds to make false license plates for their automobiles. They do not need gratuitous advice: the years are gone when Palestinian Marxists, Soviets, Cubans, or Czechoslovaks taught them the tactics of this new war. Yet they are far from self-sufficient. They must exchange information, plan their strategies beforehand, coordinate timing and objectives, and ensure their movement across borders. Thus it is not only ideological conviction but also necessity that accounts for the international character of terrorist organizations. Military training camps, special weapons difficult to get, stolen or forged documents, hiding places, lodgings abroad, regional meetings, "laundering" of cash, change of leaders, etc., are some of the mysteries underlying an intricate underground network which may never be fully revealed. Their modus operandi seems to rest on the Marxist principle of "each according to his own ability and need."

The classic cellular structure makes any type of research very difficult. This system has not only confounded the disorganized Italian police but also the efficient German security forces and their computers. In 1979 the special West German services are composed of four thousand men who, among other requirements, must have a certain educational background, be skilled in self-defense, and be "elite" sharpshooters. Engineers, physicists, and other professionals are required for certain functions. Yet in spite of all these improvements, a German official stated that their secret service could, sooner or later, infiltrate any espionage system, but that trying to do so in the Red Army was out of the question. However, this cellular organization does not make its groups self-sufficient, and has an increasing tendency toward joint action—the most spectacular coups in recent years have been notably multinational. In this regard, a British officer said that the increase in the percentage of mixed terrorist activities—German cooperation with the Red Brigades, the Japanese, and/or Palestinians—was a very serious problem, and ended by warning that if there was no high terrorist command yet, it could be in the making.

Nearly a decade ago, when European terrorism was just coming into existence, guidelines for action were established by South American, Palestinian, and Irish guerrilla groups. In the mid-1970s all known German terrorists had been trained in various centers. Members of the Red Brigades were also trained outside the peninsula. Alberto Francheschini, a Communist militant for several years before he joined Curcio, spent one year in Czechoslovakia, and at least three other leaders of the Red Brigades were also there for several months. Others were trained in North Africa and at the private "club" of terrorist headquarters in Paris. Under the management of the famous Venezuelan known throughout the world as "Carlos the jackal," the office soon promoted a multinational terrorist trade. Hundreds of youths were trained for this new type of war in camps in Africa and Asia Minor by the Dutch Red Aid, the Japanese Red Army, the Iranian National Front, the Turkish Liberation Popular Army, and others. Periodic meetings helped coordinate the work of this multinational. The first meeting was held in Lebanon in 1972; the last, in Cyprus in 1977. Germans, Japanese, Iranians, Turks, and Irish were present at both meetings. In 1976 during one of the meetings they decided to assume the responsibility of training and providing arms and financial aid to the Basques in Spain and the Bretons and Corsicans in France. It is no accident that the Spanish terrorists have imitated their style to carry out an attack against an army general last summer, or that the rate of murders performed by Basque revolutionaries should have increased geometrically. The same could be said for the outbursts of violence by Breton and Corsican separatists or the renewal of subversion in Turkey.

International cooperation in terrorist activities has gradually become evident. In 1973, a group of Palestinians and Venezuelans kidnapped a Japanese Jumbo jet on its way to Paris-Tokyo. In 1974, the Japanese Red Army took over the offices of the French Embassy in Holland, under the supervision of "Carlos" from Paris, using grenades stolen by the Baader-Meinhof band from a United States Army warehouse located in West Germany. That same year, the Baader-Meinhof band attacked the German Embassy in Stockholm using weapons provided by an Italian who had stolen them from a Swiss official arsenal. Weapons coming from the same place appeared later on in Frankfurt, Hamburg, Barcelona, and Rome. In 1975, "Carlos" supervised a group composed of two Germans and three Palestinians who kidnapped ten Arab ministers at the OPEC office in Vienna. In 1976, a German was the leader of a Palestinian command which hijacked a French airplane forcing it to land in Uganda. In 1977, an Italian led the hijacking of a Lufthansa airplane on its way to Mogadishu with the purpose of supporting the kidnapping of Schleyer.

From the fall after the kidnapping until the following spring, German couriers were detected traveling regularly between Germany and Italy in order to arrange the details of the Moro affair. Midway between the two events there appeared two young Austrians with "burnt" money and an interesting connection. The principal character in this story is a German woman called Gabrielle Krücher-Tiedemann, and it stands as a clear example of how the international organization works. In 1970 she was a member of the June 2nd Movement. In 1975, the terrorist who kidnapped Christian-Democratic leader Peter Lorenz demanded her release. She immediately flew to Aden, and later on appeared in the training camps of Haddad in South Yemen. She returned to Europe and together with "Carlos" participated in the attack against the Arab ministers in Vienna killing three persons. Then she went to Algeria together with the captives in a special airplane provided by the Austrian government. In the summer of 1977, she was in Vienna again to organize the kidnapping of a very rich businessman, Walter Palmers, which brought in two million dollars to the organization. When the Swiss policy arrested her in December 1977 she was only carrying a small sum of money to Paris. The two Austrians who were also arrested afterwards were not carrying an important sum either, since most of the money had been sent to the Red Brigades in Italy. It was not clear whether the peninsular group needed the money or whether it would be sent to other groups: but it is reasonable to assume that they needed it for the kidnapping of Aldo Moro. The meeting held between both organizations in Zurich shortly after Gabrielle was arrested is a clear sign of connivance. Another proof is a coded document found in her possession on which the notation "Al-MO" was written under the heading "Rome." But the story of Gabrielle does not end there. Shortly before she went to Vienna to prepare the attack against Palmers, her husband, Norberto Krücher, appeared in Stockholm leading a group of twenty-nine terrorists who were arrested as they were planning to kidnap a Swedish former minister for whose freedom they would demand four million dollars. Among those arrested, there were eight Swedes, two Germans, one Greek, one Tunisian, and three Latin Americans (from Mexico and Chile).

Shortly afterwards, a Chilean killed in Italy aroused the interest of the security services. He was inside a car belonging to an Italian terrorist when the bomb they were carrying exploded and killed them both. The Chilean had gone to Italy as a political refugee, and his passport showed that he had spent a year and a half in Cuba. That connection might been viewed as accidental if by then Cuba had not already been incriminated in Europe and

Africa. In the summer of 1975, the terrorists' office in Paris had been taken over by the French police which had, moreover, been about to capture the slippery "Carlos" who disappeared after killing his assistant and two men from the French secret service. This event caused the expulsion of three Cuban diplomats from Paris as well as greater surveillance of the activities of Cuban agents on the continent.

Their modus operandi is concealed through the Revolutionary Coordination Board (JCR), with offices in Paris since 1976. This organization represents about twelve ultraleftist groups from South America, and aims at obtaining the sympathy of European democracies so that they may condemn the military and/or rightest regimes of that region. It also runs a documentation center for forged passports; gathers money to finance clandestine operations; it is connected with training camps for Latin Americans, located in Cuba; and it has been organizing a service designed to place the most skilled graduates in Europe. These camps are not new. They were opened in 1966 by the DGI under the supervision of the Soviet KGB, after the Tricontinental Conference in Havana, to "organize the international antiimperialist forces." In North Korea there are similar places where, according to the Institute of Conflict Resolution in London, twenty-five hundred terrorists have been trained. Although the existence of these "schools" constitutes no novelty, the routing to Europe of specialists trained in them is. This also demonstrates Soviet interest in increasing or focusing operations on that continent.

The countries of the Warsaw Pact are aware of this strategy. Automobiles stolen in Western Europe are carried to the East and reconditioned for the transportation of weapons. Once loaded they return to the West. West German police have already intercepted three of these vehicles belonging to Interterror. Since 1971 Czechoslovakia has been supplying weapons to the IRA, and both in that country and in Bulgaria there are hideouts for terrorists escaped from Western Europe. The most common getaway is through East Germany and Berlin. This country—or its Communist party—and Czechoslovakia have contributed 400,000 dollars, during the sixties, to the maintenance of the ultraleftist magazine *Konkret,* managed by Ulrike Meinhof and her husband Klaus Reiner Hühl. The latter declared that they periodically went to East Berlin to collect funds. Training in the use of weapons is not over either. During 1977, fifty-four courses were taught in Eastern Europe, thirty-five in the Soviet Union, eight in East Germany, four in Bulgaria, four in Czechoslovakia, and three in Poland.

One of the most significant facts in the history of Interterror is that the mysterious and slippery "Carlos the jackal" was educated in Moscow. He never obtained his degree because he was expelled from Patrice Lumumba University on account of "ruffianism and anti-Soviet activities"; a good cover if the KGB already had future plans for him. Whether or not this was the case, "Carlos" disappeared for several months and afterwards reappeared in a Palestinian camp in Jordan. Whether or not he is or was an agent of Soviet intelligence or one of its representatives in Cuban organizations may never be known. Such proof would add one more element to existing evidence which indicates that the KGB is the principal force guiding terrorism on the continent.

Although the Soviet Union has always proclaimed its aversion to terrorism, and probably does not care for the ideological extravagance of ultraleftists, it may, however, not be too upset that those groups should proclaim Moscow's treason to the international proletarian revolution. On the contrary, this attitude would lessen Soviet responsibility vis-à-vis Western governments for the actions of a terrorism which helps destabilize its opponents. Nevertheless, it would seem that in recent months Soviet leaders are changing their policy and tacitly accepting the idea that the Soviet block should help Western nations in their fight against terrorism. There could be several reasons for this strategic change, such as to avoid greater problems with West Germany (the Soviet Union's largest economic creditor); to avoid an embarrassing diplomatic position vis-à-vis the Western world; and maybe for fear of an eventual subversive action in that part of the continent under their control—an action which could be founded on national vindications or doctrinal differences. All this is possible, including the fact that the Soviets may have become aware that these organizations could escape from their control. Of course, this would only be a small annoyance to Moscow, compared to the problems which the present power, ramifications, and action of Interterror is causing to Western security services.

The results of the Moro and Schleyer affairs have not been satisfactory to the terrorists, to the extent that they are beginning to show signs of uneasiness. The Red Brigades thought that Moro's kidnapping would bring Italy to the verge of collapse. But this did not happen and what is more, the assassination aroused the repudiation and rejection of the Italian people and even of the revolutionary Left. The same can be said of the Germans. In spite of their three ferocious attempts they could not force the release of the leaders of the Baader-Meinhof band (a bloody raid upon the German Embassy in Sweden, the kidnapping and murder of Schleyer, and an airplane hijacking). The consequences were even more negative. They made people become aware of the unlimited danger they represented, remaining isolated from the population which never supported their methods. Something similar happens with Spain, where Basque terrorists have staged exceedingly violent attacks, desperately attempting to break the stability of the new post-Franco regime, favored by a fluid political situation resulting from the inevitable transition the country is undergoing.

The countries directly affected have already reacted, and there has been a concentration of efforts on the part of the governments and security services of most Western European states. The Moro and Schleyer affairs "have strengthened our collective desire to resist," said an important official in the French Justice Department. Following Aldo Moro's kidnapping there appeared a formidable counterterrorist network composed of the police forces of the countries in the Common Market plus Austria and Switzerland. The latter participated in a secret meeting with the interior ministers of West Germany and Italy, held in April 1978, where a fourfold hotline was set up by telephone, radio, and telex. A similar meeting, with the participation of the French, was held in Vienna in September 1978. According to Austrian interior minister Erwin Lanc, the purpose of this organization is to achieve a rapid exchange of information, coordinate strategies, establish personal contacts among police forces, coordinate police equipment, create a computerized data bank for Western Europe on automobile trademarks, license plates, "black" money, movement across borders, and to share knowledge and experience.

The latter includes access to extensive data, contained in West German computers, on the personal history of terrorists, their trips, dental work, blood group, hair type, fingerprints, reading habits, and even musical tastes, if any. This system would attempt to embrace terrorists of different parts of the world. But this effort does not end in the cybernetic field. Special units are being trained following the model of the command techniques of the German Leatherheads (the GSG9), whose efficiency was proved when it recaptured the airplane hijacked in Mogadishu. It also includes the exchange of technology and weapons; of information on planned attacks and kidnappings; intelligence coordination, evaluation, and recovery by means of computers; as well as knowledge of the experience accumulated by Great Britain since World War II through the struggle against Communist insurgents in Malaysia, the Mau Mau in Kenya, and the IRA in Ireland. This would explain why—although the Red Brigades said, after the unfavorable repercussions of the Moro Affair, that they would move toward total civil war deploying all their organizations in Europe—results have been adverse to their interests.

This possible reflux notwithstanding, West German officials have been warning about probable attacks against NATO leaders and military stockpiles, which brings up the thought that an eventual atomic extortion could become a disagreeable reality. However, the terrorists' determination to go for civil war could turn out to be their most serious mistake, since international terrorism inevitably brings about international counterterrorism. Recent events seem to bear this out.

Since last winter, of the twenty-eight terrorists West Germany has been most earnestly looking for, more than half have been found and arrested in different countries: Holland, Great Britain, France, Switzerland, Yugoslavia, and Bulgaria. Except for one from Great Britain and four from Yugoslavia, all have been sent to the countries which requested their respective extraditions. The inclusion of France in this list is really surprising, that of Yugoslavia still more, and that of Bulgaria simply astonishing, especially if Bulgaria acted in agreement with Moscow, as a reliable Western source has said.

If we remember that in 1977 the Baader-Meinhof band was able to find a hideout for Schleyer in French territory and that the police of that country scarcely cooperated in the search for them in Alsace—where the Germans suspected them to be hiding and where the corpse finally appeared—this new attitude would indicate that France feels no longer compelled to protect terrorists and is willing to cooperate with the rest of Europe in the fight against terrorism.

The case of Bulgaria is far more important: it could be the clearest sign that Moscow no longer wants to be compromised by uncontrollable murderers. For Interterror, such an attitude could imply a greater danger than that of applied cybernetics or of the increasing efficiency of security forces. For instance, it could imply the loss of their base of operations in South Yemen, which has been a Soviet satellite since the military takeover. Without this sanctuary, hideouts would be reduced to a few Arab countries (Iraq and Libya) and security risks would be almost unmanageable. However, Bulgaria's attitude has not been followed by any other Eastern European state. Moreover, Moscow has said nothing about a possible neutralization of the Palestinians, who are directly connected with terrorists in at least fourteen countries, including Germany and Italy.

For the time being the only true fact is that the different groups continue to frighten European nations, committing at least one murder a week and exploding several bombs. These methods do not require such an important organization as that needed for kidnapping, for example; they could imply a regrouping or else the decline of their action in Europe. There is nothing to authorize the acceptance of either of the two preceding hypotheses. What happened in Bulgaria could be a change of strategy or a simple smoke screen while waiting for surveillance to become more relaxed. An official of Great Britain's Defense Department may be right in saying that the fight against multinational terrorism may end in the final battle of the century. The possibility of avoiding it depends on the speed and efficiency of the nations which are the targets of Interterror's activities. The key factor will be the joint efforts to counterattack. The time for the "final war of Europe" has been no secret since the Red Brigades announced it in March 1978. From now on, a continent which is practically surrounded will run a race against time.

Chapter 5

Terrorism and Ideology

To state, as Henry Kissinger recently did, that terrorism is the fascism of the second half of this century, represents a great part of the truth about this subject but by no means the whole truth. It is true that the subversive methodology resembles the practices used by all fascist regimes during the first half of the twentieth century. But the "red terror" was more than an entelechy in various European national processes, including Russia before the outburst of 1917. This raises the question of to what extent—speaking of terrorism—does ideology work as an instrumental generator, or as a pretext for the daily exercise of violence whose roots are much more complex than stated in public declaration, labels, and even in the conscious beliefs of its promoters. The artificers of destruction have a common ideology: nihilism. It is not always easy to see through this phenomenon. It is proclaimed that all preexisting things must be destroyed for the benefit of the people, who have a right to build their future according to their own interests and not those of the dominant classes.

Nations tend to choose security as one of the most suitable ways to reach happiness, and when they accept a crisis it is with a view toward rebuilding that lost security. Mere stability is not enough to fulfill a human being. But to embark a nation on a dangerous course involving instability and destruction, one of these two conditions must obtain: (1) the subjection by force, with no capacity for response (neither physical nor political) on the part of the organizations in charge of repelling aggression, which would become the custodians of the repudiated system; (2) the chronic establishment of repressive lifestyles—a characteristic mostly foreign to Western Europe.

An indication that terrorist groups have no real political objectives beyond systematic violence (regardless of the fact that they are controlled by international Marxism), is the example seen in some countries where such groups began their attacks from the extreme Right and then gradually shifted to the opposite pole. In Uruguay, the Tupamaros included many of rightist origin, just as Joe Baxter, one of the founders of a pseudo ultra-Catholic rightist organization, afterwards became one of the leaders of Argentina's IV International.

If ideology seems to be a simple pretext, what has allowed this type of organization to recruit young people more or less successfully? International headquarters which coordinate and promote terrorism throughout the world are not enough to generate such adhesion. Let us analyze the social background and circumstances, within the community, of those participating in organized subversion around the world.

There are a number of issues relevant to Latin America rather than Europe: (1) Does this phenomenon gather the children of blasé, displaced, and decadent aristocrats? (2) Why does the majority of supporters of these manifestations belong to the middle classes? (3) Why is only the lumpen proletariat represented, while no unionist working class is apparent? There are indeed many of wealthy extraction who in some cases are related to native aristocracies. Members of the middle classes, especially those attending universities, are the main source of recruitment. And it is also true that no significant numbers of workers can be found in terrorist groups and, if any, they generally come from the poorest and most restricted sectors of society. Thus the common denominator among these middle-class students and intellectuals and some unskilled workers is their objective or subjective marginality within their communities.

This situation, which has attracted the concern of many scholars, has had no satisfactory answer. Since such extreme conditions as wealth and poverty are found within terrorism, it is not a phenomenon associated with a specific type of society, but rather grounded on philosophical and doctrinal principles underlying much of our civilization. Youths who are the sole beneficiaries of parental property—viewed as an end rather than a means toward higher objectives—run the risk of embracing any challenge in their search for identity, however frustrating and absurd. They are the children of boredom, or they wish a more active participation in a certain historical process, adopting attitudes they consider heroic and transcendental. The case of the middle class is not very different. The university was or is—depending on the countries and times—a permanent source of frustration—and not just because of the infiltration of terrorism. In underdeveloped or developing countries, this situation is perpetually critical. The sole prospect of becoming a lawyer and ending up in some meaningless state office; of becoming an architect and working as a draftsman or decorator; of becoming an engineer and seeing emigration as the only solution—contribute to resentment against a social order which does not clarify but rather destroys future objectives. It is not strange then that, due to the imbalance between knowledge and the options for individual and/or collective realization, subversion should emerge as a quick channel for those feelings of low self-esteem, hidden under a pseudo-altruistic world view. This phenomenon is not new. It may take the form of a different totalitarianism in external appearance, but not in its basic principles, as we shall see later on.

This analysis does not intend to justify events; it only attempts an explanation of their causes and consequences. What can be done in order that these youths choose life and not death elevated to a mystic category by ultra-leftist as well as ultrarightest subversive literature? Education should be designed to prepare the individual to live in a changing society, not in yesterday's relatively static world.

Another important characteristic of the defenders or worshipers of extremist projects—in the case of noncommunist countries—is their attack on democracy. Its flaws are magnified and it is shown as a totalitarian society where the human being is alienated and exploited. The mistakes of totalitarian societies are lessened, presenting them as liberal, democratic, and with an organization which allows man to live in an almost idyllic world. This underscores the point that the real conflict is between totalitarianism and democracy.

Totalitarianism includes, universally speaking, all

types of communism and some dictatorial police-type regimes such as those found in some Third World countries. Superficially speaking, they could be said to be rightist regimes. However, calling them "rightist" would assume an ideological sophistication which they lack. In general, they have no ideology (within a political science perspective), and in order to stay in power they do not hesitate to deal both with the United States and the Soviet Union. The most salient characteristics of these regimes are: the control exercised by the state over the individual, restrictions over any type of personal freedom, monopoly over information, and cruel methods of extermination against all those opposed to the regime. An example of this type of government is that of Idi Amin.

Nazism or fascism as a political expression of power, like that of Hitler or Mussolini, do not exist in any country of the world, notwithstanding that in many areas of the West, developed or not, their followers have increased in number for several reasons, such as the slogan of the vices and permanent failure of democracy. Regarding communism, differences between Stalinism and new forms (Eurocommunism, popular democracies, Third World, etc.) are simply quantitative and technical in nature, because there is no liberal communism. The weight of that Stalinist spirit is more strongly felt in societies not subjected to either the internal or external pressure of communism. This spirit, a mixture of Marxist-Leninist postulates and Marcusian, Third World, or leftist theories of various origins, proclaims that all the world's evils come from the developed countries of the West.

Thus appear the postulates upholding the impossibility

of improving "the system," a vague term used to classify Swedish as well as Brazilian capitalism, that of the final decades of the nineteenth as well as the twentieth century. Those supporting this position claim that it is impossible to improve things without a change in society. Of course, the same ideologues would never state that it is impossible to correct the (clear) mistakes of communist societies without a radical change, that is, abolition of the existing economic system. Such a cause-effect relation is part of a strategy to be used for capitalist societies alone.

Another of the postulates is a consequence of the preceding one: The destruction of the system is a priority. And to destroy the system implies to annihilate freedom, democracy, legitimacy, elections, pluralism of opinions and beliefs. In short, the acquired rights. Paraphrasing Marcuse, the greater the tolerance, the greater the repression. The third postulate states that the only imperialism comes from capitalism, and since the United States is the bulwark of democracy as a political form and lifestyle it must be concluded that imperialism is synonymous with that nation. It is surprising that in the past few decades, to assume all these postulates has frivolously become an intellectual and political credential among leftist circles.

Having these basic principles in mind it is easy to pursue arbitrary charges against democracy, such as that democracy is a luxury, that freedom of information is a farce, that information is used for alienation. Such phrases are the preamble for a Stalinist mentality promoting an omnipotent state ruling over amorphous masses, isolated from the world, making it possible to establish a binary society composed of the bureaucracy and party hierarchy on one side and the rest of the population on the other.

Such is the ideological struggle in countries where, for geographic or geopolitical reasons, it is impossible to impose communism by force. Otherwise, we can apply the concept Stalin expressed to Tito when they still had a common view: "Whoever occupies a territory, imposes on it his own special system as far as his army can advance." Where this maxim cannot be applied, the only way is to undermine the system trying to impose, in non-totalitarian countries, the idea that there is no authentically democratic legitimacy; that deficiences are impossible to correct and that, ultimately, there are no great differences between Holland in 1978 and Nazi Germany in 1938. Therefore, both should be identically attacked.

Although revolutionary terrorism sometimes appears to be on the opposite end of this spectrum, it is an ally of Stalinist advance, despite constant denials. There is no solution for it either in Western democratic societies— other than its destruction. From there to the apocalyptic view of "death and resurrection" as a law capable of changing and improving human societies, there is only one step. This position assumes that there is no progress, that opposition to the system must be absolute and aimed at its annihilation.

We are not referring to the guerrilla whose main objective is to liberate a national territory from an invader (such as the French marquis during World War II). We are speaking of the political terrorism which develops in countries outside the communist orbit, and which takes place because of socioeconomic insecurity and political instability; or, on the other hand, in highly developed countries such as West Germany, Japan, and the United States. The central thesis of all these groups is that nothing can be done to change society but to undertake a merciless fight against all its institutions and all its members, by all means. They also state that law is a farce and that nothing can be expected from an action included in the Social Contract. However, they appeal to law when necessary, pretending to uphold what they are in fact trying to destroy.

Another classic method is infiltration into the security organizations of the system, as happened in Colombia in February 1979, blooming into a political scandal involving the two latest presidents of that country: Alfonso López Michelsen and Misael Pastrana Borrero. The protagonist of the episode is an important retired army general, José Malallana, who had been working in the Security Administration Department (DAS), a police organization in charge of the fight against terrorism. López Michelsen had dismissed him from the service (three years before the scandal) under suspicion of cooperating with terrorist groups. The scandal was unleashed with the arrest of Tony López Oyuela, a leftist accused of cooperating with the April 19th Movement. Allegedly López Oyuela had been an agent—under orders of the M-19—in charge of paying checks drawn by a company which the extremist group used as a screen. The attorney general of the Superior Military Court, Colonel Genaro Nungo, was also involved and likewise dismissed. This proves the high degree of infiltration of terrorism into the military organizations of Colombia, without clearly showing, for the time being, the consequences such a situation might bring about in the future.

This example illustrates why, in order to defend themselves from this new and violent war, some societies are compelled to enforce exceptional laws, gradually becoming—if only temporarily—semi-authoritarian communities. This has happened to France and Italy. Freedom is slowly eroded until there is an atmosphere of illegality which makes democratic institutions less and less viable. Democracy is continually mutilited, moving closer to fascism and Stalinism.

The problem is not that terrorism moves in by way of the constitution of a new state founded on a certain social consensus. We are not dealing with a revolution. Terrorism tries to eliminate any possibility of constituting a state and achieving any consensus. Uruguayan poet Ricardo Paseyre has said: "Supporting the guerrilla does not mean trying to have a good government instead of a bad one. It simply means supporting the establishment of a police state which can turn out to be either rightist or leftist; it means to retard the course of civilization." It should not be forgotten that, in the beginning, Nazism was nothing but a bunch of armed bands engaged in spreading terror.

The most important point—beyond conceptual differences—is still the struggle between democracy and totalitarianism. There is sufficient evidence that the objective of terrorism is to destabilize democracy to achieve control. That is why communist countries can more easily come to an agreement with totalitarian regimes than with democratic ones, maybe due to their isomorphic structures. If those countries (Angola, Uganda, Ethiopa, etc.) are not communist yet, they are the most susceptible to such an outcome. Even a simple "Third World socialism" fulfills the basic conditions to "help" them become totalitarian, isolated, get arms, and depend—militarily and economically—upon the Soviet Union.

No factor should be overlooked. Any war, no matter how small, is useful, because Stalinism is aware that there no longer are isolated wars among nations. It knows that all conflicts are now international. As regards this new war which compels the world to choose between totalitarianism and democracy, we must bear in mind that the enemy's strategy is to destroy basic institutions, multiply conflicts, and thereby generate chaos. To achieve that purpose, any allies are useful and valid, regardless of their ideology, because their aim is to keep the choice between rightist and leftist totalitarianism. The rest, the ideological hegemony and domination of the world, comes by itself.

Chapter 6

Present Juncture: Role of the Two Superpowers

The Soviet Union

The new form of war introduced in the world during the last few decades is characterized by an integral strategy by means of which the Soviet Union intends to enlarge its present sphere of influence. It is therefore important to study the salient characteristics of this expansionist attitude by the Soviet block and compare them to the reaction—or lack of one—by the United States.

Since World War II, the foreign policy of the Soviet Union has aimed at ensuring the security of the benefits gained during that conflict (giving priority to its national objectives) and of those derived from its position as nuclear superpower and leader of the international Marxist-Leninist movement. That policy has two fundamental characteristics, arising from (1) superpower status, being co-leader and co-rival with the United States, being jointly liable for maintaining peace and international security; and (2) being the motor of world communism, at least until 1955, when China began to compete for leadership.

That double profile of the Soviet Union's foreign policy makes analysis difficult and complex, especially when trying to distinguish between a power policy and a policy of ideological penetration, designed to impose communism throughout the world. Although in theory these assumptions can be accurately defined, in practice they are closely related, and the national interest of the Soviet state sometimes prevails over ideological considerations and vice versa. The situation is such because the Soviet Union's strategy aims at the collapse of capitalism and its replacement with communist regimes the world over on the basis of Marxist historicism and an expansionism which paradoxically, claims opposition to any kind of imperialism.

The consequences of such strategic planning are clear: the Soviets intend, through peaceful or violent means, to come closer to the West, in the awareness that they have more to gain than to lose. Such is the fatal mistake many countries have made, especially the United States which, in Tehran in 1943, Yalta in 1944, and Postdam in 1945, allowed the Soviets' dangerous expansion and helped them become a new power with which they would subsequently have to share the whole world.

The West did not learn the lesson and the Soviet Union, with tenacity and determination, has pursued an expansionist policy, applying an unusual formula which blends territorial imperialism with ideological subjection. Under the banner of peace, coexistence, economic cooperation, technological assistance, ideological solidarity, or military aid, the Soviet Union expands its presence in the world by means of communist parties, liberation movements, or terrorism. The basis of this convergent strategy lies on Soviet insistence that the world remains bipolar, and that for this reason, it confronts two hegemonic conceptions represented by itself and the United States. This is one of the reasons for the Soviet ideological rupture with China which, being more fortunate than other countries, has discussed the principle which annulled its future possibilities with respect to an expansionist policy essentially favorable to Moscow. The cold realism of Soviet diplomacy turns out to be positive for its interests, as opposed to Washington's strategy of shared responsibilities and the shedding of it role as "gendarme of peace and democracy," which implies a serious and dangerous turn for the stability of the system.

The world is moving toward multipolarity. The problem is that, being opposed to that perspective, the Soviet Union demands negotiation on an equal level with the United States in order to take advantage of the hesitations of a rival who wants to provoke the progressive reduction of its obligations in order to transfer them to its allies. This process has multiple effects on the West. On the one hand, the Soviet Union discusses with the United States the limitation of strategic weapons, emphasizing world bipolarity; on the other hand, it acts independently in countries of Western Europe and in less developed areas of the world. Such are the contradictions of a pragmatism which has both precise and unlimited hegemonic objectives. While it controls the growth of countries within its sphere of influence, it strengthens its relations with developed nations—especially European—in an attempt to weaken their alliance with its rival super-power. It plays a game of détente with the NATO countries in order to induce the dismantling of that organization. At the same time, it strengthens the military power of the Warsaw Pact which remains an important part of its strategy. Another basic postulate insists on "the recurrent realities of World War II," an attitude which has allowed it to establish new frontiers in the treaty signed with West Germany in 1970. In exchange for that recognition, Germany obtained the possibility of economic penetration in Eastern Europe and of strengthening its technological transfer to the Soviet Union. The Soviet Union is a contradictory state. Its urgent need for rapidly becoming a superpower has compelled it to relegate some sectors of its economy for the benefit of others. It now attempts to remedy that uneven growth through the industrialized countries of Europe and Japan. Without taking into account any ideological considerations, the Soviet Union has promoted and encouraged these types of operations, which will allow it to overcome the uneven growth of its economy and at the same time attempt to weaken Western alliances.

Those boasts of tactical pragmatism imply "erasing with the elbow what one has written with the hand"—when circumstances thus advise. This is the case for Soviet relations with the less developed regions of the world, where the Soviets use all the experience of their international policy aimed at expansionism. They exploit internal contradictions, attempt to destabilize democratic governments while strengthening the totalitarian ones by means of economic, military, and technical aid, and constantly present themselves as a friendly alternative as opposed to alleged pressure or lack of understanding on the part of the West. This has yielded favorable results for the Soviets, especially in newly independent African countries with a strong animosity toward their old rulers. In the case of Latin America and within the framework of the Cuban Revolution, they started working in the region with two clear goals: (1) to use the area as an experimentation ground for Interterror, taking advantage of the weakness of Latin American democracies, their socioeconomic problems, and the "prestige" of the Cuban Revolution; (2) to compromise the security of the United States—already harmed by the Cuban case— by establishing a dangerous source of conflict on one of its sides. This expansionist vocation has and will surely add new chapters equally difficult to neutralize. Let us examine to what extent the United States is aware of this fact and whether it assumes the responsibility of leading that defense.

The United States

Throughout history there have always been one or several powers which, on account of their importance, became the leaders of a given process. In all such cases, the responsibility was great and difficult to assume. In the New York *Post* of November 23, 1943, Samuel Grafton wrote that even after granting a squirrel a certificate stating that its size is equal to that of any elephant, it would continue being smaller, and all the squirrels as well as all the elephants would know it. And vice versa. Since we are dealing with the responsibility of an elephant, we shall state, with William Fox, that they cannot do what they want, and that in a well-organized world there would be a place for elephants and squirrels and they would all live in an atmosphere of security unknown in our times. That world is within our reach, but it will be beyond our grasp if we ignore the differences between the elephants and squirrels of international politics. To ignore the responsibility of the strongest would be an absurdity rather than a mistaken appreciation; as Fox says: "In times of peace, great power and great responsibility go hand in hand." Or to quote Pascal: "Justice without force is impotent. Force without justice is tyrannical. Consequently, we must combine justice with force."

Hegemonies in the history of Western civilization can be divided according to three functions: (1) expansive, as in the case of the Roman Empire, of Spain under Charles V, or of England at the end of the nineteenth century; (2) defensive, as that of the Carolingian Empire which put a stop to Moslem expansion in Europe; and (3) hegemonies including both expansive and defensive characteristics. That is, those competing for leadership with another power, as was the case for so many wars in the Old Continent and of which World War II is the clearest example.

World War II left in its wake a conflict between two antagonistic powers, one of which—expansive—aims at absolute control. The West tends to retreat, as Arnold Toynbee pointed out thirty years ago. He stated that in this encounter between the Soviet Union and the West, spiritual initiative, though not technological control, had shifted from the West to the Soviet faction. The West cannot resign itself to this, because communism, that Western heresy which the Soviets have adopted, is regarded by the majority in the West as a perverse, erroneous, disastrous doctrine and lifestyle. Preoccupation with the decline of the West has been manifest long before. Perhaps since Spengler published, in 1924 and precisely under that title, a work which shocked all Europe. After him, reference to "the crisis of the West" has been the favorite subject of many thinkers: Hilaire Belloc, Ferrater Mora, and Toynbee, among many others.

Such an attitude could imply a positive sign. However, insistence on the problem also constitutes a troublesome symptom. Is this attitude due to a lack of faith in Western values? Does it imply that the danger is serious and that there is no one to assume a defensive role? Though Europe cannot be compared to the squirrel in our example, it cannot be considered the elephant either. That position has been reserved, for more than thirty years, for the United States, which must assume that role of the modern Carolingian Empire. This raises several questions: Does the United States have a thorough understanding of its responsibility? Besides maintaining its undeniable technological development, can it successfully face the spiritual battle proposed by Toynbee? Does it have the greatness and selflessness to realize that great historical destiny? A thorough answer to each of these questions would be very difficult indeed. However, we can attempt a better understanding of the problem with relation to the central theme of this work.

Traditionally the American nation has lived within the framework of its own frontiers, paying little attention to the rest of the world. In the beginning, it only aspired to a moderate leadership in its continent in order to avoid the increasing European influence. This attitude remained unchanged until World War I, in which the United States belatedly participated bringing about a result which, had Germany been triumphant, would have changed its future strategy. Then it tried to remain aside again, and as Fox says, that irresponsible isolation by the United States and the impotence of the League of Nations showed how the divorce between power and responsibility prepared the scene for World War II. But the appeal to neutrality was only partial, because the United States had already become too involved in world events. It was beginning to understand that the Soviet Revolution was a threat not only to Europe but also to its own lifestyle. In spite of that evidence, a great psychological preparation and a planned provocation (Pearl Harbor) were needed for Roosevelt to obtain from Congress a declaration of war.

It certainly was not the best way to assume such a responsibility. The Treaty of Yalta marks the magnitude of that responsibility in the face of the violent and astonishing Soviet advance on Europe and the Asiatic Continent. The United States begins to participate in international conflicts without sufficient diplomatic experience, and without a clear understanding that hegemonic struggles in a bipolar world imply that what one state wins, the other inevitably loses. This phenomenon has repeatedly damaged the United States ever since that famous treaty was signed. This need to participate, almost abruptly, in world problems, made it lose sight of immediate troubles and take care of conflicting situations in other parts of the world. To its active presence in Korea and Vietnam may be countered systematic losses in Latin America, disappointed at being left behind. Those countries—natural allies of the United States—became severe critics and, in some cases, even opponents of its policy, on account of reminiscences of the "manifest destiny" and "gunboat diplomacy" which characterized its strategy on the continent until the first decades of this century, and also due to its disregard of conflicting political, economic, and social issues.

Cuba became a communist outpost on the threshold of a power claiming to discuss the hegemony and validity of that doctrine. From there, it radiated a powerful focus whose most spectacular act—though not the only one nor the most effective—was Ché Guevara's attempted takeover of Bolivia, the geopolitical core of South America. Afterward, Marxism won its victory in Chile—for the first time through nonviolent means—while Argentina and Uruguay became fields of experimentation and struggle for terrorism. A very hard struggle to uphold the rights of democracy ensued. The United States reacted with lack of understanding. Instead of supporting and helping its natural allies, it criticized them on the basis of an erroneous appreciation of the situation. The majority in Latin America aimed at defending a policy of preservation of the human rights set up by the West and which terrorism was trying to remove.

The reproach is as valid for one as it is for the other. Throughout history, the worst enemy of relations between the United States and Latin American countries—especially Argentina—has been mutual misunderstanding. Did anyone try to explain that what was happening in Argentina was not the result of an internal conflict but an important link in an internationally planned strategy? In April 1978, in the middle of a campaign designed to impair the reputation of the Argentine government, I had an interview with a Gaullist and a Socialist deputy in the Latin American House in Paris. I explained several aspects of the development of events, of the atmosphere of uneasiness in the country, and the personal history of some of the most prominent leaders and ideologues of terrorism as well as their most important actions. As a result, the French politicians had a clearer view of the matter and subsequently changed the condemning attitude they had had until then. Had a greater and more coordinated effort been made, the results would have been seen much earlier. Lack of information generally leads to loose judgment which tends to harm those who should be allied to stop the dangerous offensive of Interterror.

The problem lies in that, though responsibilities may be taken as mutual, different roles generally bring about different consequences. A mistaken appreciation of the different national or continental issues which join together in the Western scheme and its allies, can become a dangerous time bomb on the very threshold of the system. Recent events in Iran compel such a reflection. Those accustomed to Marxist economic determinism and to the mistakes underlying such interpretations, must have been surprised at Zbigniew Brzezinski's scientism in the analysis of international relations. This example, taken at random, attempts to show the risks of an analysis based on a certain scheme of values, on a certain dogmatism which cannot be mechanically applied to societies as different from each other as Argentina and Iran or as the United States with respect to both of them. Such a tendency must certainly trouble those who consider the United States a leader in the survival of Western democracy. Ernest May, fifteen years ago, observed that many people from other parts of the world regard the United States as a gigantic adolescent: an immensely strong nation lacking tact, discretion, prudence, wisdom, and experience. Americans will have to become aware that responsibility for defending a certain lifestyle is not limited to their own but also that of the Western world as a whole. It is an "elephant" which, maybe against its will, has to defend a community heterogeneous in form but homogeneous in essence. In the end, its own survival will depend upon how well that defense is managed.

Since the Bay of Pigs invasion and the American retreat from Vietnam—bitter defeats— foreign policy has been an important subject within the American political debate. President Carter's decision of assuming the defense of human rights with no concessions has sometimes led him to adopt contradictory attitudes regarding his country's vital interests. To condemn the violation of human rights is an ethical and not a political problem. Since that violation is condemned as a general principle, it must be extended to all countries with no exceptions. In some cases, for instance, his silence regarding the Phillipines, Cuba or Nicaragua was somewhat dubious.

Events in Iran have made the subject bitter and the polemic has come to have unprecedented characteristics, especially because of traditional sectors in the American polity and economy which have demanded drastic measures regarding what they consider a successful Soviet offensive in the international field. Among the qualified spokesmen upholding this position, the *Wall Street Journal* has expressed disapproval of what it considers a passive and defeatist attitude. Irving Kristol, one of its columnists, defined the shah's fall as the end of an era for American foreign policy, the result of which would be the expulsion of American power from the Middle East as a whole. He viewed this as a consequence of the management of foreign relations by decadent Wilsonians dominated by an evangelic idealism and a strict legalism, as opposed to whom, those self-defined as stubborn realists demanded the use of American power and a strengthening of the CIA, which nowadays can do nothing because the government lacks the will to participate in a direct military intervention.

Regarding this attack, historian Arthur Schlesinger pronounced himself in favor of the Carter administration. He stated that the idea that the United States could have saved the shah by means of the CIA and sending an expeditionary force was too extravagant to deserve consideration. He added that after Vietnam, all that was needed to persuade the world of American weakness and incompetency would have been to participate once more in a civil war in the Third World on the side of the losing party. He concluded that in that case Kristol would have been right when he stated that the nations of this world admire winners and not losers or even good losers.

There are problems created by the policy of indiscriminate intervention which traditional American groups subscribe to. The first mistake is that they consider the interests of the United States as identical regardless of geographic locale. Schlesinger is correct in saying that extreme universalism would make American intervention in all conflicts inevitable, ultimately leading to an absurd position.

This approach is the result of two mistaken evaluations: to regard all adverse events as successes for Moscow, when this is not always the case, and to underestimate the nationalist trends in countries of the Third World. An event adverse to the United States does not always imply a triumph for the Soviets, although sometimes immediate appearances may seem to indicate it. For example, the overthrow of a government friendly to the United States by a nationalist coup d'état, generally leads the new rulers to seek Moscow in order to obtain weapons and even certain economic benefits especially important in certain political circumstances; sometimes this attitude makes everyone think that the nation has become a new satellite of Moscow. However, it may not be the case. The mistake arises from failure to understand nationalism as an important emotional factor in both domestic and international policies in the present era. Contradicting all socialist forecasts in favor of an internationalism which would defeat nationalist trends—expressions of the bourgeoisie—the twentieth century has seen nationalism advance and grow throughout the world, including in states within the communist orbit, whether Soviet or Chinese. Due to a lack of understanding on the part of the United States, nationalist leaders have occasionally been forced to adopt Marxist slogans in order to obtain weapons and economic resources from the Soviets.

These factors must be taken into account by the United States in order to be more successful in the management of international policy. For example, it must begin to recognize the importance of nationalist trends in a Third World overwhelmed by problems but unwilling to renounce its self-determination, even at the cost of certain temporary concessions in order to obtain benefits which would otherwise be impossible to achieve. The United States must determine where its permanent interests lie and who are its natural allies in order to establish priorities, and settle when and where its intervention is justifiable and the limits of such intervention.

It is not a matter of disregarding the existence of great men who knew how to interpret and assume that terrible responsibility. But neither should we ignore the enormous doubts as to the challenge which must be assumed and a real lack of awareness about the dangers which such hesitation could bring about. Among those who had a clear view of the problem were John F. Kennedy and Harry S Truman who, in 1950, explained that in today's world we are facing the danger that the increasing demand for freedom and higher standards of living may be corrupted and betrayed by the false promises of communism. In its merciless struggle for power, communism takes advantage of all the imperfections of our system and the fact that many democratic nations are slow in their efforts to secure a better living for their citizens. He added that for the United States that challenge was more than military. It was a challenge to the honesty of its profession of democratic faith; to the efficiency and stability of its economic system; a challenge to its willingness to work with other nations toward world peace and prosperity.

Kennedy stated in 1961 that all nations should know, whether they loved the United States or not, that for the sake of the survival and triumph of freedom the people would pay any price whatsoever, bear any burden, suffer any hardship, support any friend, or oppose any enemy.

Kennedy understood the role and the responsibility—the enormous responsibility he had to assume. That view of the historical process allowed him to appreciate the importance of the part which Latin American countries would play, as natural allies of the United States and forming a security fence to stop Soviet advance. In referring to them he pointed out that to the brother republics on the south, the United States made a specific promise: to make good on its word by means of a new alliance for progress; to help free men break the chains of poverty. He added that this peaceful revolution of hope could not become a prey to hostile powers. That neighbor nations should know that the United States would join forces with them to resist aggression or subversion in any part of America. And that any other power should know that this hemisphere would continue being the head of its own household. Kennedy said that the United States was neither omnipotent nor omniscient, that it merely represented 6 percent of the world's population, that it could not impose its will upon the remaining 94 percent of humanity, that it could not correct all wrongs or cure all adversities, and that therefore there could not be a United States solution for all world problems.

The day when this is clearly understood, the image of the United States will probably attain the stature and outlook its best leaders desire, and surely also then it will find itself more efficiently defending its own and authentic interests together with the destiny of freedom and democracy in the world. Perhaps in light of past events we should now remember these concepts with a frank spirit of self-criticism and with the firm intention of retaking a road which has already been mapped out and which threatens to close itself forever.